Reiki Heart Blessing Training Book

Wonderful new way of using the healing power of Reiki

Designer and Author - Billie Topa Tate

Reiki Heart Blessings

Training Book

Designed by Billie Topa Tate, Mescalero Apache

8th Degree Reiki Master Teacher

Table of Contents

About The Author

Billie Topa Tate, Mescalero Apache is the founder of MSI Wellness Center in Evanston, Illinois. She is also a Reiki Master Teacher 8th degree and has been teaching for the past 20 years.   She maintains her successful practice within the MSI Wellness Center and her vision is to "Create a Sacred Space One Person at a Time" which is her vision statement for her wellness center. She brings the reader into the wonderful Native American world of healing through many of her books. She writes and shares ancient stories, powerful healing practices and wisdom mentoring that has never been shared with the general public before.   Within this book you will find fresh new wisdom and fresh new ways of using our reiki practice.

Billie invites the reader to understand how to create a sacred sanctuary within ourselves by using the Reiki Heart blessing techniques.   Also, how to use the Reiki Heart Blessings for groups of people, animals, plants, trees, and ourselves and so much more.

Enjoy this book as a wonderful guide to the healing power of the heart center and Reiki which awakens and celebrates the true spirit of who we are.

Acknowledgements

I wish to thank all my wonderful teachers who have guided me throughout my life. Since the time of my youth they have guiding me with great patience and understanding – thank you so very much. I will always remember your great presence and continue to share the Creator's wisdom at all times. I also, wish to express my deepest gratitude to my wonderful daughter Monique Little Doll, she has inspired me with her beauty, grace, wisdom and support, Namaste to you dearest daughter. I am so glad we are walking this journey together as mother and daughter. To my beautiful Mother, Mama Little Wolf, who has been my most loving teacher and mother. My heart sings to have been blessed with both my mother, Mama Little Wolf, and my wisdom filled father Papa Little Wolf. Papa Little Wolf has shown me so much wisdom throughout all trials and tribulations. My deepest gratitude to my loving husband-Neil who has been by my side not only supporting my efforts, but also providing his wonderful energy to help me create and develop our MSI Wellness Center. My deepest appreciation and love to Neil.   Also, to all my wonderful students who have taken the time to help empower the world with their kindness, peace and wisdom.

INTRODUCTION

Reiki Heart Blessing Training

Newly designed and Authored by Billie Topa Tate

Welcome to the Reiki Heart Blessing Training Book

This book is designed for people who are attuned to the Reiki symbols and received the Reiki training. However, the lay person can still use the Reiki Heart Blessing with the suggested energy based applications instead of the Reiki symbols.

I am so happy to share this training with you. I created this powerful platform of using Reiki and mystical anatomy to help all sentient beings connect with their goodness and to share that goodness with others. When I first starting teaching approximately 20 years ago, I took 10 percent of the credit for what I shared. Now that I have walked this path of teaching and sharing for many years, I have always said to my students that I take 2 percent of the credit for what I do, teach and share. My teachers in spirit, holy medicine people and all the wonderful beings who have assisted me in virtuous ways are the ones who guide me and share their wonderful wisdom through me to the people of the world.

Enjoy, experience and provide the healing power of the Reiki Heart Blessing which promotes relaxation and de-stresses the body.

Billie Topa Tate is a Reiki Master Teacher 8th degree and has designed and provide this specialized   Reiki training.

A Reiki Heart Blessing can be provided for your clients, family, students and can also be a wonderful addition to your list of services. It is an exciting special step by step training regarding a personalized Reiki Heart Blessing which activates an abundance of positive energy within our heart chakra. This helps our clients, students, family members and ourselves to initiate wonderful self-care and helps launch a joyful energy within our energy field. Reiki heart blessings can be done and received any time, especially when someone needs a beautiful energy hug.

Our heart center is truly structured to give and receive unconditional love. These days we are experiencing a deficiency in the vitamin, many call vitamin "H." Vitamin "H" being the vitamin and vitality of "Hugs."   This Reiki Heart Blessing training is a great way of fulfilling the need for the vitamin "H" deficiency.   Our heart is built to provide compassion, divine love, peace, understanding and so many other wonderful virtues. But when you combine this with the healing power of Reiki, it is very empowering indeed.

CHAPTER 1

What is a Reiki Heart Blessing

"Energy work is like a blessing to our Spirit" Billie Topa Tate

A Reiki Heart Blessing is a wonderful fresh new application of our Reiki tradition. Many of our loved ones, friends and co-workers have been experiencing stress. When we experience chronic stress we can sometimes forget our own goodness. A Reiki Heart Blessing applies Reiki to what is called in the Native tradition "The Column of Light" which is along the spine. This "Column of Light" is a great source of assimilating wonderful virtuous energy throughout the body and chakras. "The Column of Light" is often used during the Reiki Attunement to bless each chakra with the Reiki energy and Reiki Symbols. Having said this, the Reiki Heart Blessing also uses the "The Column of Light" as a wonderful dispersing of congested energy and also an infusion of the healing energies of Reiki for the purpose of infusing the body, mind and spirit with virtuous energy. Thus, providing a great remembrance of goodness that we all have and so much more.

The Reiki Heart Blessing lifts the spirit of our family, friends, animals and our wonderful self as we add this to our energy tool kit.   Like gold for our spirit – the principle of goodness is such a blessing to us.   Add to this the upper regions of our heart center with the healing power of the Reiki Heart Blessing which combines the healing vibration of reiki.   This is the perfect time to learn and provide this wonderful Reiki Heart Blessing, which gently empowers and lifts the spirit of our families, friends, companion animals, plants and our wonderful self.

The Reiki Heart Blessing activates the vibrations of goodness and peace within the heart center and then allows for the quality of goodness and peace to infuse the entire energy field.

CHAPTER 2

The Reiki Heart Blessing Invocation

"A focus of virtuous intention with the power of words is good medicine for the world"

Billie Topa Tate

Our Native tradition guides us to begin all teachings, ceremony and healing energies with a sacred intention, a prayer or a heartfelt invocation for our virtuous elders and virtuous teachers to help us, guide us and provide healing medicine for our earnest efforts.

You are welcome to use the Reiki Heart Blessing Invocation before you begin the application of the Reiki Heart Blessing.   If you are administering the Reiki Heart Blessing to a group of people, you only need to say this invocation one time for the day

Reiki Heart Blessing Invocation

Designed by Billie Topa Tate

By the power of my good merits, I invoke for my virtuous Reiki lineage, Grand Master Dr. Usui, Grand Master Takata, Grand Master Hayashi and all the wonderful beings who assist me in virtuous ways.   Please provide your wonderful wisdom, virtuous guidance, healing energies for my Reiki Heart Blessings today.   I am super receptive, super conductive and I accept this virtuous energy for my healing practice and Reiki Heart Blessings I provide everyone today.   Bless me and everyone who receives a Reiki Heart Blessing divine wisdom, healing energies, peace, happiness and for a great remembrance of our own goodness.   Bless us so we can be a blessing to others.   Here and now and from this day forward, physically, mentally, emotionally, spiritually and at all other virtuous levels.   In full faith so be it now.

CHAPTER 3

Reiki Heart Blessing to a Group of People

"Our great purpose in life is to share virtuous energy with others" Billie Topa Tate

Step by Step Procedure

It is always good to provide a Reiki Heart Blessing after a meditation so that everyone feels lifted and balanced in their energy field.

1) Provide ample time at the end for a sharing of their feelings and or experiences.
2) Do a wonderful Reiki Invocation or if you do not know Reiki you can say a wonderful sacred intention before you start.

3) Secure that all chairs are positioned in a circle which helps everyone feel comfortable. Make sure that you have ample room behind every person.

4) Welcome all participants to the meditation and explain that when you are facilitating the Reiki Heart Blessing - you will be standing behind them. It is easier to facilitate the Reiki Heart Blessing when people are sitting in their chairs. But, if they prefer to sit on the floor you can do the Reiki Heart Blessing from a distance. If there are too many people to sit in one circle set up an additional outer circle.

5) Pass a basket of paper and pencils, you can also do a fancy scroll with a little bow or tie string and a pencil, so everyone has time before meditation to write down a blessing that they are requesting. A good example is to invoke for a wonderful blessing for their life or for someone they love. The piece of paper or scroll will always be in their possession. They can take it home to continue to focus on their written intentions.

6) Ask each participant to place the scroll on their heart during the Reiki Blessing or in between their two hands on their lap. This will help them stay connected to their heart center and their wonderful intention.

7) Facilitate a 20-minute meditation and then ask each participant to keep their eyes closed while you do the Reiki Heart blessing. If they do not feel comfortable keeping their eyes closed, this is fine.   The reason why we ask them to relax and keep their eyes closed is, when we close our eyes, we are accessing our inner world and during meditation when we close our eyes, we are accessing our spirit.

8) Use soft nature music while each participant relaxes during the Reiki Heart Blessing.

9) Please wear your sanitary mask and white gloves if you will be placing your hands on their shoulders during the Reiki Heart Blessing. During our COVID 19 virus protocol, it is important that we follow social distancing and or wearing a mask.

10) You will be placing your hands very gently on the tops of their shoulders or if they feel uncomfortable, you can certainly just stand next to them as you send them a Reiki Heart Blessing. The reason why we are using their shoulders is the following: The shoulders mystical represent a place where people sometimes place their stress and the concept of burden.   When we allow the shoulders to relax and release, we are helping the person feel a great lifting of heavy energy. Here is the Reiki Heart Blessing Technique….

11) Firstly, during meditation please request that your wonderful divine helpers bless you with healing energies so that you can facilitate this energy to all the people that you provide the Reiki Heart Blessing.

12) Start clockwise and very gently place your hands on the shoulders of the first person (or stand behind them) focus on their crown chakra, the top of their head and the front and the back of the heart.   While you are focusing on these areas send the five reiki symbols into the crown (if you do not know the five reiki symbols just invoke for virtuous reiki and divine light to flow through you and empower the person with virtuous peace and virtuous happiness) and allow the symbols to remain in the heart center. See the heart center become filled with light.   If you do not know the Reiki symbols, simply see the golden words of divine peace and divine happiness in the heart center and the crown center

13) Send happiness peace, joy and safety as a thought into the crown center and see these energies floating gently down to the heart center. See these as words in their heart. See the heart center become filled with light.   Take some time to allow the person to assimilate this wonderful energy.

14) Then just internally say I asked for virtuous angels to continue to provide this person with divine peace and divine happiness.

15) Allow for wonderful energy to flow through you to the person. Say Reiki on… and allow the reiki to flow through you to the person. Take your time with this process.

16) Ask for the virtuous angel in the heart center to awaken, ask for virtuous self-love and unconditional love to awaken in the person's heart center.

17) If you know the five Reiki Symbols, send them into the shoulders and ask for all worry to be transformed into peace and virtuous wisdom. If you do not know the five Reiki Symbols – ask for the angel of peace to help this person to release all worry and replace it with peace and virtuous wisdom.

18) Express gratitude for this wonderful opportunity to be of service.

19) Then cut the energy cord with your mind and move to the next person

20) When you are all done, thank them very much for participating in the heart blessing, invite them to share starting clockwise with the first person you provided the Reiki Heart Blessing and then close the circle with a short gratitude statement. Congratulations you completed the Reiki Heart Blessing for a group.

CHAPTER 4

Reiki Heart Blessing to One Person

"The Heart Center is where we can activate the golden light of the Creator" Billie Topa Tate

A Reiki Heart Blessing can be done for our family, friends, co-workers and general public. Following this procedure to provide Reiki to one person is a perfect way of helping lift congested energy off the energy field and thus providing a balance of happiness and general wellbeing.

Step by Step Procedure

1) Use soft nature music while the person relaxes during the Reiki Heart Blessing.
2) Please wear your mask and white gloves if you will be placing your hands on their shoulders during the Reiki Heart Blessing.
3) You will be placing your hands very gently on the tops of their shoulders or if they feel uncomfortable with being touched, you could certainly just stand next to your student or family member as you send them a Reiki blessing
4) Here is the Reiki Heart Blessing Technique….
5) Take time to request that your wonderful divine helpers bless you with healing energies so that you can facilitate this energy to your student or family member that you will be providing the Reiki Heart Blessing.
6) Very gently place your hands on the person (or stand behind them) focus on their crown chakra and the front and the back of the heart, then send the five reiki symbols into the crown (if you do not know the five reiki symbols just invoke for virtuous reiki and divine light to flow through you and empower the person with virtuous peace and virtuous happiness) and allow the symbols to remain in the heart center. See the heart center become filled with light. If you do not know the Reiki symbols, simply see the golden words of divine peace and divine happiness in the heart center and the crown center
7) Send happiness peace, joy and safety as a thought into the crown center and then in the heart center. See these as words in their heart. See the heart center become filled with light
8) Then just internally say I asked for virtuous angels to continue to provide this person with divine peace and divine happiness.

9) Allow for wonderful energy to flow through you to the person

10) Ask for the virtuous angel in the heart center to awaken, ask for virtuous self-love and unconditional love to awaken in the person's heart center.

11) If you know the five Reiki Symbols, send them into the shoulders of the person receiving the reiki blessing and ask for all worry to be transformed into peace and virtuous wisdom. If you do not know the five Reiki Symbols – ask for the angel of peace to help this person to release all worry and replace it with peace and virtuous wisdom.

12) Express gratitude for this wonderful opportunity to be of service

13) Then cut the energy cord with your mind.

14) When you are all done, thank them very much for participating in the heart blessing, invite them to share as an option. Then close with a short gratitude statement.

CHAPTER 5

Reiki Heart Blessing to a Companion Animal

"Animals are physical angels that try their best to teach us unconditional love"

Billie Topa Tate

Animals sometimes move around during energy sessions and we want them to feel comfortable doing so.   When you are administering the Reiki Heart Blessing to your companion animal you are welcome to do so physically or from a distance.   When you are sending energy from a distance, just see the companion animal in your mind's eye and go through the motions of sending the Reiki Heart Blessing.

<u>Step by Step Procedure</u>

1) Focus on the crown chakra also, the front and the back of the heart. Then   send the five reiki symbols into the crown (if you do not know the five reiki symbols just invoke for virtuous reiki and divine light to flow through you and empower your wonderful companion animal with virtuous peace and virtuous happiness) and allow the symbols to remain in the heart center, by visualizing the symbols in the heart center. See the heart center become filled with light. If you do not know the Reiki symbols, simply see the golden words of divine peace and divine happiness in the heart center and the crown center

2) Send happiness peace, joy and safety as a thought into the crown center and then in the heart center. See the qualities of peace, joy and safety as words in their heart. See the heart center become filled with light

3) Then just internally say I ask for virtuous angels to continue to provide this wonderful companion animal with divine peace and divine happiness.

4) Allow for wonderful energy to flow through you to this wonderful companion animal.

5) Ask for the virtuous angel in the heart center to awaken, ask for virtuous self-love and unconditional love to awaken in the wonderful companion animal's heart center.

6) If you know the five Reiki Symbols, send them into the shoulders of the companion animal and ask for all worry to be transformed into peace and virtuous wisdom. If you do not know the five Reiki Symbols – ask for the angel of peace to help this companion animal to release all worry and replace it with peace and virtuous wisdom.

7) Express gratitude for this wonderful opportunity to be of service

8) Then cut the energy cord with your mind and give your pet a big
   hug. When you are all done, express gratitude for this wonderful
   moment in time

CHAPTER 6

Reiki Heart Blessings to a Plant or Tree

"The Plant Kingdom is the kingdom of healing forces, through physical and emotional healing medicines they so wonderfully gift to us" Billie Topa Tate

We call the plants and trees, the Green Nation.   We would not survive without them. They are wonderful advocates for us and are very much alive. I feel it is important to acknowledge the plants and trees also, empower and bless them.   They do many good things for us and many within the human kingdom do not even know they exist and help us in so many ways. I am happy we have this chapter, which can truly connect us with them.   This is a good start to establishing a wonderful spirit connection with them and getting us closer to our enlightenment through honoring our extended families within the Green Nation.

Firstly, ask permission to step into the energy field of the plant or tree by saying "I am asking permission to enter your energy field."   You will feel a welcoming energy or if you feel the plant or tree said no, then wait for another time.

<u>Step by Step Procedure</u>

1) Focus on the top of the plant or tree (the top of the tree or plant is the crown center of the plant) and the base of the plant or tree (is the heart center for the plant).   Send peace and gratitude energy first. Then send the five reiki symbols into the crown – which is the top of the plant or tree and the center of the plant or tree (if you do not know the five reiki symbols just invoke for virtuous reiki and divine light to flow through you and empower the plant or tree with virtuous peace ad virtuous happiness) and allow the symbols to remain in the heart center. See the heart center become filled with light.   If you do not know the Reiki symbols, simply see the golden words of divine peace and divine happiness in the heart center and the crown center

2) Send happiness peace, joy and safety as a thought into the crown center, which is the top of the plant and then in the heart center. See these as words in their heart. See the heart center become filled with light

3) Then just internally say I asked for virtuous angels to continue to provide this wonderful plant or tree with divine peace and divine happiness.

4) Allow for wonderful energy to flow through you to this wonderful plant or tree

5) Ask for the virtuous angel in the heart center to awaken, ask for virtuous self-love and unconditional love to awaken in the wonderful plant or tree heart center.

6) If you know the five Reiki Symbols, send them into the plant or tree and ask for peace and virtuous wisdom for the plant or tree. If you do not know the five Reiki Symbols – ask for the angel of peace to help this plant or tree to have peace and virtuous wisdom.

7) Express gratitude for this wonderful opportunity to be of service

8) Then cut the energy cord with your mind's eye and give the plant or tree a big hug

CHAPTER 7

Reiki Heart Blessings to Ourselves

"The best medicine we can gift the world, is the medicine of patience and love for ourselves." Billie Topa Tate

We all can benefit from a blessing in our body, mind and spirit.   The Universe, The Great Spirit, our loved ones on the other side and our virtuous helpers want very much to have opportunities to provide healing energy to us.   A Reiki Heart Blessing for ourselves can be done first thing in the morning and also during the day when a boost of happiness and healthy vitality is needed.   Below is the step by step process and many blessings to you.

Step by Step Procedure

1. Secure at least 30 minutes of uninterrupted time
2. Relax and take a nice deep breath in through you nose and exhale through your mouth several times.
3. Get comfortable and settle into a place where your body feels comfortable and supported
4. Close your eyes if possible.   Closing our eyes allows us to access our inner world and also access our wonderful energy world.
5. If possible, please say this wonderful energetic narrative out loud
6. "By the power of my good merits, I invoke for my virtuous teachers in spirit, virtuous holy medicine people, my personal guardian angels, my virtuous divine helpers and all the wonderful beings who assist me in virtuous ways.   I ask for you to bless my crown chakra which is at the top of my head with the empowering reiki symbols. The angel of wisdom within your crown chakra will allow for this wonderful reiki energy to gently float into my heart center through my column of light.   I wish to remember my goodness, remember my wonderful purpose, and refresh my body, mind and spirit with your divine intervention. Bless me so I can be a blessing to others. Bless me with wisdom, peace, healing, happiness and prosperity. I am super receptive and super conductive and accept this wonderful energy to flow through me at all levels.   Physically, mentally, emotionally, spiritually and at all other levels. Here and now and from this day forward, in full faith so be it now. Thank you.
7. Next, send wonderful peace and light to your crown chakra, and see all the reiki symbols floating into your crown center.

8. Next, see this wonderful energy and reiki symbols, floating into the column of light along the spine and gently positioning into the heart center.
9. Allow for this wonderful energy and reiki symbols to remain in your heart center, and allow for your breath to be connected to nature.
10. Visualize the trees, the clouds, the mountains, the water, grandmother moon, father sky and the sun.   Connect and send blessings to all aspects of nature.
11. Visualize your entire body being filled with beautiful light, peace, wisdom and the reiki symbols.
12. Allow for your breath to be peaceful and calm
13. Express gratitude and see all the energy helping you and ask for what you need to relieve your stress or concerns.
14. Then gently come back into your awareness of your surroundings and very gently open your eyes.
15. Express gratitude one more time and if you have time, write into your reiki journal your thoughts and experiences.

CHAPTER 8

Integrating Reiki Heart Blessings into my Reiki practice

Our reiki practice in itself is an excellent way to provide healing energy to our clients, family, friends, companion animals and even our plants. I grow my own sprouts and normally when you buy sprouts in the supermarket there are approximately 3-4 inches in length. I enjoy applying reiki to the soil and the seeds of my sprouts and also during the process of growing them. When I harvest them, they are approximately 10-12 inches long and very delicious. This demonstrates the wonderful healing power of our intention and reiki.

One day I was teaching the Reiki Heart Blessing in our classroom at our MSI Wellness Center, when one of my students asked a great question. Can we integrate the Reiki Heart Blessing into our regular Reiki Sessions or even in our massage practice?   The answer is yes, we can.   There are several recommendations to accommodate the Reiki Heart Blessings.

Step by Step procedure

A) Use your intuition and apply the Reiki Heart Blessing during a quiet moment within the Massage applications.   Review with your client the process so that your client will feel comfortable and at ease with the reiki application.

B) Apply the Reiki Heart Blessing right before the massage session. This will help your client go into a deeper aspect of rest and releasing tension.   It would be advisable to review the Reiki Heart Blessing process with your client and even place the Reiki Heart Blessing within your list of services and add a short narrative regarding the benefits, such as, deep relaxation. I have found that many of my clients energetically participate in a deeper more meaningful way when we have discussed the application of the Reiki Heart Blessing.

C) Before you start your reiki session, take time to administer the Reiki Heart Blessing to launch your reiki session in a deeper way for your client.   However, experiment and see if your clients enjoy the Reiki Heart blessing at the end of a reiki session as well.

CHAPTER 9

Taking Time to Allow a Person to Share their Healing Process

"Sharing our feelings and thoughts can help our inner universe find peace through the power of words" Billie Topa Tate

During the time you are administering the Reiki Heart Blessing, please take time to be sensitive to the recipient assimilation of this healing energy.

Sometimes the person will be releasing trauma or images which were blocks and obstacles to their healing and happiness.

Often, I have noticed people releasing emotions, physical involuntary muscle releases and images floating up to the sky or being taken by angels. Please be respectful and gently hold the space for them. Sometimes people just need a quiet healing moment rather than talking and sharing with you or the group. Try your best not to share what you saw or experienced during their time of release as this may take away from their healing experience. When we are facilitating reiki we often see or feel the images they are releasing. However, it is highly important to not make it about what we see or feel but rather respectfully hold the space of the individual and honor their quiet time.

Also, if you feel the person needs extra time to share please allot this time. Sometimes people feel uncomfortable sharing because they have not had time to process their experience.   We need to honor this process as well.

If you feel your client or student needs an extra cleaning of their energy field. You are welcome to use the invocation in chapter 13. Which Invokes for the reiki angels to take all energies that are impinging on the happiness of the recipient to receive medical care in the energy world and ask for your reiki helpers to replace the energy with peace and wholeness.

CHAPTER 10

Adjusting our Energy Field with a Mantra

"Our energy field is a wonderful energy tools, a gift from the Creator to use to navigate energy."

Billie Topa Tate

In our native tradition we were taught about our energy field.   Mainly, the energy field is a mystical tool, a gift from the Creator.   One of our life lessons is to learn how to navigate our energy field. Also, to learn how to facilitate energy and the various qualities of energy through our energy field.   In general, we are learning how to move energy through us.   Our energy field is under our dominion, in addition to providing healing to our past lives that we requested to work with in this lifetime. We also are aspiring to become enlightened through the new experiences and events within this lifetime.

When we are applying the Reiki Heart Blessing, we are using our wonderful energy field, our powerful intention and the healing power of our hands, which channels the reiki energy. Our hands are also wonderful energy tools which are an extension of two very important chakras. The chakra of the heart and the chakra of the throat. You will notice that when you extend your hands outward, your hands are right in between your heart and your throat center.

I have found that my energy field can facilitate more of the reiki energy when I use the enclosed mantra. You do not have to say it out loud, you can use your internal voice. Each time we use our voice and the power of words we are adjusting our energy field to accommodate the intention of our words.

Here is the mantra to adjust your energy field when you are applying the Reiki Heart Blessing.

"I am super receptive and super conductive and accept this virtuous healing energy to flow through me"

You can also use this mantra to adjust your energy field when you are applying healing energy at any time. Try this within your Reiki energy sessions.

CHAPTER 11

Mystical Anatomy, Why the Crown Charka

"The energy centers we call Charkas are also called the Encasements by the Native Elders, which means they encase past lives that we are providing healing and wholeness for in this lifetime."

Billie Topa Tate

People often ask why we are applying the reiki symbols into the crown chakra (which is the top of the head) instead of just applying them directly into the heart center.   The reason why we use the crown center to apply the reiki symbols is directly connected to the principle of the "Column of Light." Within many of our Native stories we were taught about the "Column of Light" along the spine.   Which helps us stay connect to our higher self and our spirit guides but also allows for healing energy and wisdom to integrate into our spine, our nervous system, our charkas and so much more.   This beautiful channel of light is a wonderful way to allow for the Reiki symbols and Reiki energy to gently float into the crown center and then gently travel and flow to the heart center.   "The Column of Light" has the permeability quality of unconditional love and is much better suited to receive and also assimilate wonderful energy into the chakras and move gently into every aspect of our energy field.   This is part of our mystical anatomy.

Reiki can never harm anyone or anything and having said this, sometimes when people experience trauma.   There is a possibility they may carry it energetically within the body, such as the heart region, the shoulders and or the digestive area.   Also the chakras, especially the heart charka. If we apply reiki directly to that area where trauma may reside it may be such a different energy sensation that it may cause the person to feel distracted by the different energy.   This is another reason why we use the "Column of Light" during the application of the Reiki Heart Blessing.

CHAPTER 12

Keeping a Reiki Journal

"Journaling is where our spirit and our personality can speak to each other and thus insights can occur." Billie Topa Tate

A reiki journal can be your most useful tool and I recommend you keep one for all your observations, ideas and field work experiences.   You will also notice there are times your higher self, your guides and your reiki helpers will provide great insights within your notes.

As Reiki Practitioners we understand that Reiki is a healing technique based on the principle that the reiki practitioner will channel universal life force energy by means of touch, intention and application of reiki symbols. This is done for the purpose of promoting a natural healing process for the client and thus helping restore wellness within the client. Having said this, we become more insightful and proficient when we keep notes of our learning experiences during our reiki sessions and use them as learning tools to possibly apply in the future to other upcoming clients.

Another general recommendation is to use your reiki journal during meditation practice to write profound insights and recommendations you receive for your life's journey. This helps us to utilize our life experiences much more profoundly.

I like to keep my reiki journal with me at all times so when I am facilitating reiki I can write down my experiences and new protocols that come to me after reiki sessions.

Your energetic notes can be your most profound tools. I also like to gift a reiki journal to clients to help them utilize this tool for great insights and resolution thoughts.

CHAPTER 13

Slowing Down The Process So People Can Release

"Holding a respectful honoring space for people, animals and plants is like God sending a blessing through us" Billie Topa Tate

During the Reiki Heart Blessing please take time to allow for your client and or student to gently release. Sometimes they can experience involuntary muscle releases which equate to releasing some aspects of emotions or images from the past. My teacher use to say, the issues are in the tissues and I could not agree more. During your field work you will experience many different situations regarding the release of energy. I always like to clean the energy of each person I will be working on. This is important so any congested energy gets released and makes room for the wonderful positive healing energy through your reiki application.

You can use the following narrative to clear the energy field of your client before you apply the Reiki Heart Blessing.

By the power of my good merits, I invoke for my virtuous teachers in spirit, my reiki divine helpers and all the wonderful beings who assist me in virtuous ways.   Please provide your wonderful assistance and remove all harmful energies that may be impinging upon the wellbeing of this person (if you know the person's name please say their name here).   Take these harmful energies to receive medical care in the energy world and fill the void from which they were removed with divine and virtuous peace and divine and virtuous wisdom. Here and now and from this day forward, physically, mentally, emotionally, spiritually and at all other levels. So be it now   thank you.

Use this wonderful clearing invocation as often as you like.

CHAPTER 14

Endless Reiki Blessings

"Wisdom comes from expressing a desire for it"   *Billie Topa Tate*

Firstly, it is an honor to spend this time with you. My book provides a rare glimpse into the energy world of the Mescalero Apache. Sharing the power, wisdom and native techniques which I applied to The Reiki Heart Blessing training. My book will guide and mentor the reader not only to utilize these wonderful energy tools but also to bring the value of these principles and techniques into our life's journey. I am looking forward to your application of this wonderful new way of applying reiki. Please consider some of my other books, such as, "The Book of Sacred Wisdom – the writings of a medicine woman. But also, "The Smudging Ceremony" by Billie Topa Tate which will be available soon through amazon books and kindle.

Billie Topa Tate, Mescalero Apache brings the reader into the wonderful Native American world of healing. She writes and shares ancient stories, and also within her book called "The Smudging Ceremony" shares powerful smudging practices and wisdom mentoring that has never been shared with the general public before.   Within this book you will find ideal and extremely useful smudging ceremonies to clear our homes of negative energy, elevate and restore our spirit, help lift depression, promote harmony and empowers us to use fresh wisdom and fresh energy tools to bring healing into our life. She introduces us to the Green Nation - the plant kingdom and why we use certain ceremonial plants for the Smudging Ceremonies.

In Closing, I would like to thank you for sharing this time with me and enjoy this book as a wonderful guide to the healing power of Reiki which awakens and celebrates the true spirit of who we are.

Endless Reiki Blessings to you,

Billie Topa Tate
Mescalero Apache
Founder
MSI Wellness Center 2144 Ashland Suite 1, Evanston, Illinois 60201
msi-healing.com   also follow us on Facebook "MSI Wellness Center"